# Extreme Places
# The Darkest and the Brightest

## KATIE MARSICO

Children's Press®
An Imprint of Scholastic Inc.

**Content Consultant**
Injeong Jo, PhD
Assistant Professor
Department of Geography
Texas State University
San Marcos, Texas

Library of Congress Cataloging-in-Publication Data
Marsico, Katie, 1980– author.
The darkest and the brightest / by Katie Marsico.
    pages cm. — (A true book)
 Summary: "Learn all about the darkest and brightest places on Earth and find out what it takes
for life to survive in these extreme locations."— Provided by publisher.
 Includes bibliographical references and index.
 ISBN 978-0-531-21848-8 (library binding) — ISBN 978-0-531-21787-0 (pbk.)
1. Extreme environments—Juvenile literature. 2. Sunshine—Juvenile literature. 3. Night—Juvenile litera-
ture. 4. Barrow (Alaska)—Juvenile literature. 5. Andes—Juvenile literature. I. Title. II. Series: True book.
 GB58.M366 2016
 551.6—dc23                                          2015011265

All rights reserved. Published in 2016 by Children's Press, an imprint of Scholastic Inc.
Printed in the United States of America 113
SCHOLASTIC, CHILDREN'S PRESS, A TRUE BOOK™, and associated logos are trademarks and/or
registered trademarks of Scholastic Inc.
1 2 3 4 5 6 7 8 9 10 R 25 24 23 22 21 20 19 18 17 16

**Front cover: Front cover (main): Anglerfish**

**Front cover (inset): The sun
shining on Death Valley**

**Back cover: Northern lights glowing
above Alaska's White Mountains**

# Find the Truth!

**Everything** you are about to read is true *except* for one of the sentences on this page.

Which one is **TRUE**?

**T or F**  Both polar night and polar day occur in Barrow, Alaska.

**T or F**  Bright lights have little effect on wildlife.

Find the answers in this book.

3

# Contents

THE **BIG** TRUTH!

**American
kestrel**

Well-Adapted Animals

4

In very dark places far from city lights, a person can see the Milky Way at night.

About 15,000 miles (24,000 kilometers) of neon tubing light Las Vegas.

The sun inches above the horizon in Barrow, Alaska, after months of darkness.

# CHAPTER 1

# From Dark Valleys to Shining Cities

Starting in November, residents of Barrow, Alaska, soak up their last glimpse of sunlight for months. During that time, the sun remains below the horizon. That's the line at which Earth's surface and sky appear to meet. For up to 10 weeks, Barrow seems bathed in endless **twilight**. The long darkness makes it difficult for some people to distinguish one day from the next.

 Barrow, Alaska, is the northern-most city in the United States.

# From One Extreme to Another

Anyone passing through the highest parts of the Andes Mountains will face entirely different challenges. In this South American mountain range, the powerful **tropical** sun and high **elevation** result in extreme brightness. The light reflecting off the snowy peaks can be intense. Sometimes, it even causes a form of vision loss called snow blindness. Fortunately, snow blindness is temporary and is usually preventable.

**The sun can be particularly intense in the high elevations of the Andes Mountains.**

**Dark skies make it easier to observe the stars and other objects in the sky at night.**

Not everyone wants to shield their eyes from extreme brightness. Some scientists, for example, want to observe the **illumination** of cities from outer space. Others, by contrast, seek out the darkest, clearest night skies on Earth. Then they gaze upward to view clusters of stars shining amid the extreme darkness.

**The sun's bright light plays an important role in life on Earth.**

# A Closer Look at Light

Several factors contribute to extremes of light. The sun is one. The star at the center of our solar system is an immensely powerful source of natural light. Artificial light, which people often produce with electricity, is another. Organisms— including people—depend on light to survive. The balance between brightness and darkness has a huge impact on many aspects of life, from sleep patterns to stargazing.

Living in extreme darkness or extreme brightness can be challenging. In certain situations, it is even dangerous. Over time, people and other organisms have **adapted** to the levels of light in their environments. Along the way, they have experienced extremes that are occasionally risky but often are also a wonder to behold.

**It's important to protect your eyes with sunglasses in bright sunlight.**

ACE

DOG IRON RANCH, OKLAHOMA 3246 MI.

DOMINICAN REPUBLIC 4955 MI.

6464 MI. CHIAPAS MEXICO

BARRO

The sun sets in Barrow at the
beginning of a long polar night.

# Never-Ending Night

For Barrow, Alaska, 51 to 67 days of every year blend into one long night. This period is known as polar night. Polar night happens near the North and South poles, within areas called the polar circles. These are a pair of imaginary lines, called latitudes, circling the globe parallel to the equator. The equator is located at 0 degrees latitude, around Earth's middle. The polar circle near the north pole is the Arctic Circle. The polar circle in the south is the Antarctic Circle.

# Tilted Planet

Polar night happens because Earth's axis tilts, or slopes. The axis is the imaginary line through the center of Earth, around which the planet rotates, or spins. It takes approximately one year for Earth to orbit, or circle, the sun. As it does, the angle of the axis affects how much light different parts of the world receive. Polar night happens when the ends of the axis—the poles—point away from the sun.

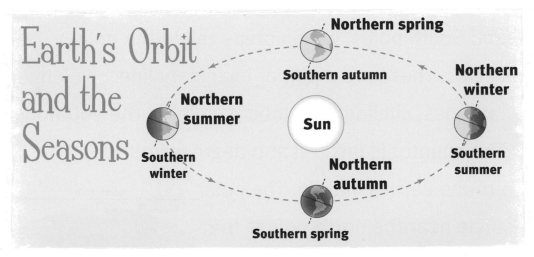

**Earth's Orbit and the Seasons**

Northern spring
Southern autumn

Northern winter

Northern summer

Sun

Southern winter

Northern autumn

Southern summer

Southern spring

**The angle at which the sun's light hits Earth determines the seasons. Winter happens in Earth's northern hemisphere, or half, when the North pole points away from the sun. Then, the sun's light hits the northern hemisphere less directly, providing less energy.**

**In Norway, which stretches above the Arctic Circle, the sun is sometimes visible at night.**

The polar circles, nearer Earth's poles, are positioned at a greater tilt both toward and away from the sun. They therefore experience more extreme changes in light. These include periods of polar night as well as polar day, when the sun remains visible for longer than 24 hours at a time. During polar night in the Arctic Circle in the north, polar day is happening within the Antarctic Circle in the south. The opposite is also true.

Fortunately, people have come up with ways to cope with the challenges of polar night. In Barrow, some residents use bright-light therapy to cope with the long darkness. They sit near a box that produces an artificial version of the natural light normally found outdoors. Others schedule trips to sunnier destinations during the months of November, December, and January.

**Light therapy can help resolve the issues caused by long periods of darkness.**

# Understanding SAD

In locations such as Barrow, the lack of sunlight puts residents at risk of suffering from seasonal affective disorder (SAD). People with SAD experience depression, or extreme sadness, because of the changing seasons and light patterns. This condition typically begins in fall and lasts through winter. Symptoms of SAD range from moodiness and fatigue to trouble concentrating and sleeping. Treatment includes medication, light therapy, and counseling.

The Andes are the longest
mountain chain in the world.

Hikers in the Andes
Mountains must deal
with both bright light
and cold temperatures.

# CHAPTER 3

# Brutal Brightness

When people picture the world's brightest locations, they often envision warm, sun-kissed beaches or deserts devoid of shade. So they might be surprised to learn that the most extreme brightness is actually found amid snow-covered peaks. High up in the Andes Mountains, the rays of the sun are among the most intense in the world. According to scientists, they are especially powerful throughout Peru, Bolivia, Chile, and Argentina.

Andes Mountain Range

Peru

Bolivia

Chile

Argentina

**The highest peaks of the Andes reach into the clouds.**

# Up High in the Andes

One reason the sun's rays beat so brightly on certain parts of the Andes is the mountains' elevation. The average elevation of the range is approximately 13,000 feet (4,000 meters) above sea level. At higher elevations, Earth's atmosphere becomes thinner. Normally, gases and particles in the atmosphere absorb some of the energy of the sun's rays. The thinner atmosphere in the high mountains means that less of that energy is absorbed—and more sunlight gets through.

The Andes' geographical location also plays a role in the extremely bright conditions there. Portions of the mountain range lie in the tropics, a region near Earth's equator. The tropics receive more intense sunlight because they face the sun more directly than areas closer to the polar circles do. Sometimes the sunshine in this region is so bright it can even create risks to people's health.

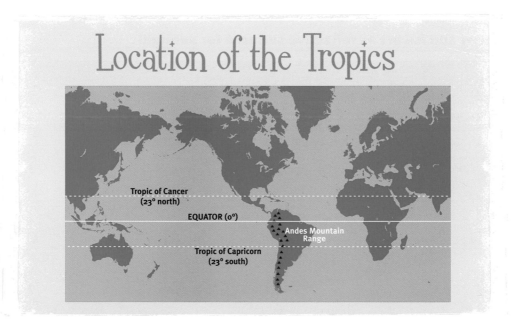

**The tropics are between about 23 degrees north latitude and 23 degrees south latitude.**

# Blindingly Bright

Sunburn and snow blindness are among the risks people face in snowy, sunny regions. The surface of the snow acts almost like a mirror. It reflects the sun's light, including invisible ultraviolet (UV) rays. Though UV rays can't be seen, they contain high levels of powerful energy. This energy is strong enough to burn someone's skin and eyes.

**Snow and ice act as reflective surfaces for sunlight.**

**Sunglasses or goggles can prevent snow blindness.**

Usually, a person suffering from snow blindness experiences pain, redness and swelling of the eyes, and sensitivity to light. However, this condition can also trigger a more frightening symptom—temporary vision loss. The good news is that, like sunburn, snow blindness is preventable. People spending time in extremely bright, snowy conditions should take certain precautions. These include using sunscreen and wearing either sunglasses or snow goggles.

# Well-Adapted Animals

From under the sea to high in the air, some animals must live with extreme darkness or brightness. To survive in these environments, they have evolved amazing adaptations.

## Undersea Light Show

Far beneath the ocean's surface, the sun fails to penetrate. In response to the dark, some animals simply make their own light. The firefly squid is one organism with this ability, called bioluminescence. Organs called photophores produce a bluish light. Firefly squid use this glow both to communicate and to distract predators.

## Patches with a Purpose

The bright sun of the Sonora Desert in the southwestern United States doesn't stop American kestrels from flying. Black patches under the birds' eyes help absorb sunlight. This prevents brightness from reflecting upward and impairing their vision. Outdoor athletes often smudge black grease called eye black under their eyes to create the same effect.

## Amazing Eyelids

How do animals in sunny, snowy environments avoid snow blindness? Polar bears depend on an extra pair of eyelids that are translucent. Because some light passes through them, a polar bear still detects movement. Much like sunglasses, however, these eyelids filter out extreme brightness. This feature protects the bear's eyes from the glare of sunlight reflecting off the snow.

## Terrific Tentacles

Star-nosed moles are nearly blind. Still, eyesight isn't much use to them anyhow. These mammals live in underground tunnels and therefore rely heavily on their sense of touch. They "feel" their way through their environment using 22 tentacles with specialized sensory organs.

The Atacama is home to
six observatories.

# CHAPTER 4

# The Best Stargazing on the Planet

Once the sun sets in Chile's Atacama desert region, an amazing transformation occurs. The desert landscape is cloaked in shadows, but the night sky comes alive with countless glistening stars. Stargazers from across the globe flock to the Atacama to stare up in wonderment. It is one of several night skies throughout the world recognized for being both extremely clear and extremely dark.

Atacama Desert

**The Milky Way is clearly visible in the night sky above New Zealand's South Island.**

# Pitch-Black Perfection

Exceptionally dark skies also draw stargazers to Namibia, New Zealand, and Ireland. There are several reasons these areas provide incomparable views of the stars. In some cases, the high elevation and thinner air offer a clearer view up above. In others, a dry atmosphere doesn't support cloud cover that would conceal, or hide, the nighttime darkness.

Locations with extremely dark night skies also have little to no light pollution. Light pollution happens when artificial lights contaminate, or spoil, the darkness that naturally occurs after the sun sets. Streetlights, car lights, and lighting used in homes and businesses all contribute to the problem. By artificially illuminating an otherwise blackened sky, these lights make it more difficult to observe the stars and planets.

**Light pollution often makes it difficult for people in big cities to see stars.**

Light pollution is why you can't see many stars in densely populated cities. Skies without light pollution tend to be far from **urban** areas. Most of the populated areas within the Atacama are small farming or mining communities. As a result, a limited amount of artificial light shines into the desert. This combines with the Atacama's high elevation and lack of clouds to set the stage for extreme darkness at night.

**There is very little light pollution in the Atacama Desert because few people live there.**

Observatories contain powerful telescopes and other equipment for observing the stars.

## Saving Dark Skies

Since the 1980s, groups such as the International Dark-Sky Association (IDA) have formed to help reduce light pollution. Their goal is to preserve, or save, the extreme darkness people depend on to observe the stars. For astronomers, who study objects in space, extremely dark skies represent an invaluable learning opportunity. That is why locations such as the Atacama are home to several major **observatories**.

**Canada's Mont-Mégantic International Dark Sky Reserve is one of the areas where dark skies have been placed under protection.**

A large part of the IDA's efforts involves identifying parks, reserves, and communities that feature extremely clear, dark skies. Currently, the IDA has noted 38 parks, 9 reserves, and 10 communities around the world. They can be found across North America, New Zealand, Namibia, and parts of Europe. Many more places are also working to be recognized by the IDA.

# Limiting Lights

Thanks to a growing awareness of light pollution and the problems it creates, people in many places are working to limit it in their communities. Simple steps include turning off lights when they're not being used. Light-pollution experts also recommend that home and business owners pay special attention to outdoor lighting. Picking lights that produce the least amount of glare is another way to preserve dazzlingly dark night skies.

Vast numbers of lights on the ground make the outlines of North and South America clearly visible from space.

# Lights Seen From Space

Light pollution may spoil the view for stargazers. But for astronauts gazing back at Earth, it creates bright spots on the planet that can be seen even from space! The extreme brightness of cities such as Las Vegas, Nevada, has been described as a kind of "human footprint." From space, this footprint is proof both that people live on Earth and that they can alter their environment.

♀ Las Vegas,
Nevada

# The Brightest City on Earth

Across the globe, extreme brightness shapes the identity of several major cities. Lights from casinos, hotels, and constant traffic are among Las Vegas's best-known features. In Paris, France, the Eiffel Tower is equipped with 20,000 lightbulbs. These bulbs sparkle for five minutes an hour every night. From Chicago, Illinois, to Tokyo, Japan, there is a long list of urban areas that set the planet aglow.

**Las Vegas, Nevada, is famous for its bright, colorful lights.**

**The lights of Las Vegas outline the layout of the city's streets.**

Astronauts can use the light patterns in these locations to identify various cities from space. The National Aeronautics and Space Administration (NASA) and the National Oceanic and Atmospheric Administration (NOAA) have obtained special satellite images of Earth. They reveal what the planet looks like at night. After reviewing the images, experts proclaimed Las Vegas to be the world's brightest spot.

**The lights of the Eiffel Tower are a defining feature of the night sky of Paris.**

# Amazing or Overpowering?

Yet for some people—not just stargazers—too much artificial light is both annoying and overpowering. For starters, it puts a strain on resources used to produce electricity. In addition, extremely bright lights sometimes disrupt healthy sleep patterns. Scientists believe they also interfere with the natural production of certain **hormones**. Humans rely on these chemicals in the body to grow and stay healthy.

Extreme brightness takes a toll on wildlife as well. Scientists have learned that artificial light disrupts birds' normal flight patterns. Sea turtles are threatened by extreme illumination, too. These endangered reptiles come ashore at night to lay their eggs. However, artificial lighting near or along beaches distracts and confuses them. In response, sea turtles frequently turn to other nesting sites that aren't as safe for either their eggs or their newly hatched babies.

**Newly hatched sea turtles make their way into the water at night.**

41

Of course, people depend on a certain amount of artificial light. Many people try to balance the need for brightness with what's best for human health, wildlife, and the environment. Some people use blackout shades and sleep masks. These reduce the impact of nighttime illumination on their sleep cycle. Others work to protect animals—for instance, by trying to limit lighting in areas where sea turtles nest.

**Many coastal communities where sea turtles nest keep street lights off during the months when the turtles lay their eggs.**

**This image captured by an astronaut aboard the International Space Station shows the bright lights of Florida and Louisiana.**

# Incredible Extremes

The deep polar night of Alaska, the dazzling starlit skies of the Atacama Desert, and the intense glare of the sun in the Andes Mountains and of the lights of Las Vegas are are all unique. The extreme light and extreme darkness of these areas are the source of both awe-inspiring beauty and significant challenges. And, whether extremely dark or extremely bright, these places reflect the infinite ways in which humans and other organisms adapt to the world. ★

**Length of the annual period of polar night in Barrow, Alaska:** Up to 10 weeks

**Average height of landforms within the Andes Mountains:** 13,000 ft. (4,000 meters) above sea level

**Location of the strongest UV rays ever recorded on Earth:** Licancabur Volcano in the Bolivian Andes

**Height above Earth from which various city lights have been viewed and photographed:** 516 mi (830 km)

**Number of parks, reserves, and communities recognized by the IDA worldwide:** 57

**Number of lightbulbs used to illuminate the Eiffel Tower in Paris, France:** 20,000

Did you find the truth?

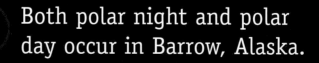
Both polar night and polar day occur in Barrow, Alaska.

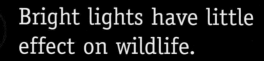
Bright lights have little effect on wildlife.

# Resources

## Books

Aloian, Molly. *The Andes*. New York: Crabtree Publishing, 2012.

Peppas, Lynn. *The Atacama Desert*. New York: Crabtree Publishing, 2013.

Silverman, Buffy. *Let's Investigate Light*. Vero Beach, FL: Rourke Publishing, 2012.

Sparrow, Giles. *Night Sky*. New York: Scholastic, 2012.

**Visit this Scholastic Web site for more information on darkest and brightest places:**
★ www.factsfornow.scholastic.com
Enter the keywords **Darkest and Brightest**

# Important Words

**adapted** (uh-DAPT-id) — changed over time to fit in better with the environment

**elevation** (el-uh-VAY-shuhn) — the height of something above sea level

**hormones** (HOR-mohnz) — chemical substances made by the body that affect the way an organism grows, develops, and functions

**illumination** (i-loo-muh-NAY-shuhn) — the lighting up of something

**observatories** (uhb-ZUR-vuh-tor-eez) — special buildings that have telescopes or other instruments for observing and studying the stars or the weather

**sensory** (SEN-sur-ee) — of or having to do with the senses, namely sight, smell, hearing, taste, and touch

**translucent** (tranz-LOO-suhnt) — not completely clear but allowing some light through

**tropical** (TRAH-pi-kuhl) — of or having to do with the hot, rainy areas of Earth near the equator

**twilight** (TWYE-lite) — the time when day is ending and night is beginning, after the sun has set and before it is dark

**urban** (UR-buhn) — having to do with or living in a city

# Index

Page numbers in **bold** indicate illustrations.

# About the Author

Katie Marsico graduated from Northwestern University and worked as an editor in reference publishing before she began writing in 2006. Since that time, she has published more than 200 titles for children and young adults. Ms. Marsico hopes to find some extremely clear, dark night skies and go stargazing with her children.